ITALY TRAVEL GUIDE 2023 TUSCANY

Uncovering The Best of Tuscany, Insider Tips for Your 2023 Italian Adventure

PIUS BORR

Table of contents

PART I

INTRODUCTION

The central Italian area of Tuscany is well known for its breathtaking scenery, rich cultural history, and delectable cuisine.

Tuscany, a region rich in history and culture and home to cities like Florence,

Pisa, and Siena, offers visitors the chance to immerse themselves in the Renaissance, wander through ancient towns, and savor world-class wines and cuisine.

For travelers looking for the finest of Tuscany in 2023, this travel guide is intended to offer expert advice.

This guide will provide useful tips and ideas for discovering Tuscany's must-see sights, hidden jewels, and distinctive experiences, whether you are planning your first trip to Italy or are an experienced traveler eager to discover new locations.

In addition to providing an overview of the region's key attractions, cultural and gastronomic experiences, and outdoor activities, this book also provides information on the geography, climate, and transportation options of Tuscany.

We'll also offer insider advice on how to organize your vacation, what to anticipate while traveling, and where to stay in Tuscany.

Whether you're looking for outdoor experiences, art, and culture, or just a quiet vacation, Tuscany has plenty to offer everyone. With the help of this guide, you can adjust your Tuscany itinerary to suit your interests and preferences, making sure that your trip to Tuscany is one you won't soon forget.

Pack your luggage and get ready to explore Tuscany at its finest in 2023. Your go-to resource for exploring everything that this area has to offer will be this guide.

Reasons why Tuscany Should Be On Your Travel Bucket List

The central Italian region of Tuscany is renowned for its stunning scenery, extensive history, and mouthwatering cuisine. Here are some of the explanations as to why it ought to be on every traveler's bucket list:

- **Scenery**

With its endless expanse of rolling hills, vineyards, and olive orchards, Tuscany has some of the most beautiful landscapes in all of Italy. A photographer's paradise, the area is also filled with charming hilltop towns, medieval castles, and antiquated ruins.

• Food and Wine

Tuscan cuisine is renowned for being straightforward, filling, and delectable. Fresh, regional ingredients like tomatoes, beans, bread, and cheese are used to make Tuscan cuisine, which is frequently coupled with the region's world-famous wines.

The renowned   and pasta dishes like pappardelle with wild boar ragu are some of the most well-liked foods in Tuscany.

The top wineries in Italy are located in Tuscany, where wines like Chianti, Brunello di Montalcino, and Vino Nobile di Montepulciano are produced.

- **Culture and History**

There are many museums, art galleries, and historical places to visit in Tuscany, which is rich in culture and history. Some of Italy's most well-known Renaissance works, including works by Michelangelo, Botticelli, and Leonardo da Vinci, are found in this area.

A must-see destination for art enthusiasts is Florence, the capital of Tuscany, which is home to the Accademia Museum and Uffizi Gallery, two internationally renowned museums.

The majestic Cathedral in Florence and Siena's medieval walls are just two examples of the architectural marvels found in Tuscany.

- **Hospitality**

Tuscany is renowned for its hospitable residents who are always willing to share their customs and culture with visitors. Many agriturismo, or farmhouses that provide lodging, food, and experiences like wine tastings and cooking workshops, can be found in the area.

An excellent approach to becoming fully immersed in the Tuscan culture and enjoying the hospitality of the area is to stay at an agriturismo.

- **Outdoor Activities**

There are numerous options for horseback riding, cycling, and hiking across Tuscany, making it a haven for outdoor enthusiasts.

There are numerous spas in the area where you may unwind and revitalize in the natural hot springs. With stunning beaches like Cala Violina and Spiaggia delle Rocchette, Tuscany's coastline is a well-liked vacation spot for beachgoers.

In conclusion, Tuscany is a place that everyone should visit once in a lifetime. Tuscany has something to offer every traveler with its breathtaking beauty, delectable cuisine, and wine, rich history and culture, warm hospitality, and limitless outdoor activities. So prepare for a memorable vacation in 2023 by packing your luggage!

PART II

GETTING TO KNOW TUSCANY

The central Italian region of Tuscany has a total area of over 23,000 square kilometers. Ten provinces, each with its history, culture, and scenery, make up the country. Everything you should know to begin learning about Tuscany is as follows:

- **Geographical overview**

The regions of Emilia-Romagna, Marche, Umbria, and Lazio, in that order, border Tuscany to its north, east, south, and southeast, as well as the Ligurian Sea to its west, the Apennine Alps to its north and east, and the Ligurian Sea to its west.

Firenze, Arezzo, Grosseto, Livorno, Lucca, Massa and Carrara, Pisa, Pistoia, Prato, and Siena are the ten provinces that make up the region.

The beautiful landscapes of Tuscany, which include rolling hills, vineyards, olive groves, and cypress trees as well as its coastal regions and mountain ranges, are well known.

Tuscany experiences scorching summers and mild winters due to its Mediterranean environment.

Tuscany is best visited in the spring (April to June) and fall (September to November), when the weather is nice and there are fewer tourists around. Summer (July to August) is the busiest travel season, therefore many tourist destinations and cities may be crowded.

The low season in Tuscany runs from December to March, but if you like skiing, winter sports, or cultural events, it might still be a terrific time to go.

- **Transportation options for getting around Tuscany**

Florence Airport, Pisa International Airport, and Grosseto Airport are the three primary airports in Tuscany. Major airlines offer both domestic and inteinternationalvices at all three airports.

With important rail lines linking Florence, Pisa, and Siena to other regions of Italy, Tuscany is also reachable by train.

Getting around Tuscany by renting a car is a popular choice because it enables you to travel to smaller towns and rural areas. Yet, parking can be hard to come by, and driving in cities can be tricky.

Buses are a good way to navigate throughout Tuscany and there is a good network of them. Additionally, several towns and cities have bike rental shops or bike-sharing programs, which may be a fun and environmentally beneficial way to explore.

You'll be more prepared to organize your vacation and navigate the region once you arrive in Tuscany if you are familiar with the geography, climatic conditions, and transportation options of the region. After learning these fundamentals, you'll be prepared to enter Tuscany and begin discovering its numerous riches.

PART III

TUSCANY'S MUST-SEE ATTRACTIONS

Tuscany is home to a wide variety of spectacular landmarks, including iconic works of art and architecture, charming villages, and breathtaking natural settings. You won't want to miss any of the following sights when you travel to Italy in 2023:

- **Florence**

Firenze, the seat of Tuscany and the cradle of the Renaissance is the location of some of the most renowned works of art and architecture in the entire world. The famous Cathedral, the Uffizi Museum, and the Accademia Gallery, which is home to

Michelangelo's David, should not be missed.

The medieval heart of Florence, a UNESCO World Heritage site, may be explored by strolling across the Ponte

Vecchio, going to the Boboli Gardens, and more.

- **Siena**

Siena is a must-see location in Tuscany because of its magnificent Gothic architecture and medieval charm. The Siena Cathedral, the Palazzo Pubblico, and the Piazza del Campo should not be missed.

Discover the ancient center's meandering streets, indulge in some of Siena's delectable cuisine, and take in the lively ambiance of the city.

- **Pisa**

Pisa, which is famed for having the world's most iconic leaning tower, is a well-liked vacation spot. Yet Pisa is more than just its well-known tower; make sure to also check out the Cathedral and Baptistery.

Enjoy the vibrant street markets, great seafood specialties, and a promenade along the Arno River while in Pisa.

- **In San Gimignano**

San Gimignano is a charming medieval village that has stood the test of time and is recognized for its recognizable towers.

The Collegiate Church, the Palazzo del Popolo, and the Civic Museum should not be missed.

Have a gelato in the Piazza della Cisterna while strolling through the town's winding lancs and admiring the breathtaking views of the surrounding countryside.

- **Area of Chianti Wine**

Some of the most well-known wines in the world originate in Tuscany, and wine aficionados must travel to the Chianti region. Visit one of the many local wineries, taste some of the famed Chianti Classico, and take in the breathtaking views of the surrounding rolling hills and vineyards.

These are just a few of Tuscany's numerous must-see sights. Tuscany has plenty to offer everyone, whether they are interested in the beautiful scenery, delectable food, and wine, or history and culture. To experience the best of Tuscany in 2023, make sure to include these top attractions on your itinerary.

PART IV

FOOD AND WINE IN TUSCANY

In addition to its breathtaking vistas and extensive history, Tuscany is recognized for its delectable cuisine and top-notch wines. Here are some must-try Italian dishes and beverages for your 2023 travels:

- **Tuscan food**

The use of fresh, high-quality ingredients and simplicity are two characteristics of Tuscan cuisine. Don't pass up the renowned Bistecca alla Fiorentina, a thick piece of steak seasoned with salt and olive oil and grilled over an open flame.

Other foods you should try are Pici, a sort of handmade pasta served with a variety of sauces, and Ribollita, a hearty soup made with bread, beans, and vegetables.

- **Wine**

Some of the most well-known wines in the world, such as Chianti, Brunello di Montalcino, and Vino Nobile di Montepulciano, are produced in Tuscany. To sample these delectable wines, go on a wine tour and stop by one of the numerous vineyards in the area.

Don't forget to sample Grappa, a potent alcohol created from grape pomace, as well as Vin Santo, a sweet dessert wine made from sun-dried grapes.

- **Public Markets**

The local markets are one of the best places to enjoy Tuscan cuisine. A must-see location in Florence is t

he San Lorenzo Market, which provides a huge selection of fresh fruit, meats, cheeses, and other regional specialties.

Another excellent choice is Florence's Mercato Centrale, which features a sizable indoor market with a wide selection of foods and beverages. Visit the Piazza del

Mercato in Siena to find a variety of regional goods, including cheeses, cured meats, and wines.

- **Kitchen Classes**

There are lots of cooking classes offered in the area for individuals who want to learn how to make Tuscan food. Learn how to make pasta from scratch, cook typical Tuscan foods, or even brew your wine by enrolling in a class.

Any traveler to the region must sample the cuisine and wine of Tuscany. Tuscany has much to offer everyone, from the renowned wines to the delectable cuisine produced with fresh, premium ingredients.

Prepare to sample the finest of Tuscany in 2023 by including these gastronomic experiences on your schedule.

Guide to Tuscany's Wine Regions And Top Wineries

With so many distinct wine regions and wineries to select from, Tuscany is known for its wine, making it challenging to know where to begin. In case you're planning an Italian vacation in 2023, here is a tour of Tuscany's wine regions and some of the best wineries to check out:

- **Chianti**

One of Tuscany's most well-known wine districts is Chianti, which is renowned for its red wine produced mostly from the Sangiovese grape.

The best Chianti wineries to visit include Felsina, Castello di Ama, and Castello di Volpaia.

- **Montalcino**

Another well-known wine region in Tuscany is Montalcino, which is well-known for the Sangiovese-based Brunello di Montalcino wine.

Il Palazzone, Casanova di Neri, and Poggio di Sotto are a few of the best wineries to visit in Montalcino.

- **Montepulciano**

Despite being a lesser-known wine region in Tuscany, Montepulciano is still well worth a trip for its Sangiovese-based Vino Nobile di Montepulciano wine.

In Montepulciano, the best wineries to visit include Poliziano, Avignonesi, and Salcheto.

- **Bolgheri**

A seaside wine region in Tuscany called Bolgheri is well-known for its Super Tuscan wines, which are produced from a combination of Sangiovese and other grape varietals.

Ornellaia, Sassicaia, and Le Macchiole are a few of the best wineries in Bolgheri to explore.

- **San Gimignano sangria**

A white wine region in Tuscany called Vernaccia di San Gimignano is well-known for its Vernaccia di San Gimignano beverage.

At Vernaccia di San Gimignano, the best wineries to visit include Panizzi, Fattoria di Fugnano, and Il Colombaio di Santa Chiara.

Tips for Visiting Wineries in Tuscany

When visiting vineyards, make appointments in advance, especially in the busy summer months.
To secure your safety while traveling and to make the most of your visit, think about hiring a driver or joining a guided tour.

Enjoy the countryside and the wineries' hospitality while taking your time. Several wineries provide restaurants and lodging in addition to tours and tastings.

Tuscany's wine regions and wineries offer something for every wine enthusiast, from world-renowned red wines to lesser-known white wines.

Be sure to add a wine tour to your itinerary and discover the best of Tuscany's wine country in 2023.

PART V

ART AND CULTURE OF TUSCANY

Tuscany is an area rich in culture, history, and art. Tuscany is a place that will excite any art and culture fan, from the legendary works of Michelangelo and Leonardo da Vinci to the breathtaking architecture of Florence and Siena.

For people who are interested in Tuscany's art and culture, the following places and activities are a must-see:

- **The Uffizi Art Gallery**

One of the most well-known art museums in the world, the Uffizi Gallery, is situated in Florence, the regional capital of

Tuscany. The museum is home to a sizable Renaissance art collection that includes creations by Botticelli, Michelangelo, and Leonardo da Vinci.

The museum also houses some of the most well-known works of art in existence, such as "The Birth of Venus" by Botticelli and "Annunciation" by Leonardo da Vinci.

• Academe Gallery

Another well-known art gallery in Florence is the Accademia Gallery, which is best known for housing Michelangelo's "David," one of the most well-known sculptures in the entire world and a must-see for anybody interested in art and sculpture.

• The Leaning Tower of Pisa

One of Italy's most recognizable structures, the Leaning Tower of Pisa is situated in the Tuscan city of Pisa. Visitors can climb to the top of the tower, which is known for its unusual tilt and offers breathtaking views of the surroundings.

- **Cathedral of Siena**

One of Italy's most stunning buildings, Siena Cathedral is found in the Tuscan city of Siena. The church is well-known for its beautiful mosaics and paintings inside as well as its gorgeous facade of black and white striped marble.

- **Villa Vecchia**

One of Florence's most well-known landmarks is the medieval palace known as Palazzo Vecchio, which is situated in the city's center. Vasari's frescoes and Michelangelo's statues are among the most beautiful works of art and architecture in Tuscany to be found in the palace.

- **Italy Wine Tours**

A wine tour is a fantastic way to learn about the history, culture, and traditions of

Tuscany, which is equally well-known for its wine.

In addition to learning about the wine-making process, several wineries provide guided tours and tastings where guests may savor some of the region's well-known wines, including Chianti and Brunello di Montalcino.

In conclusion, Tuscany is an area that is rich in culture and art, with a variety of experiences and attractions for any art enthusiast.

Tuscany's art and culture are likely to leave an indelible impact on any tourist, from well-known museums and landmarks to breathtaking cathedrals and palaces. Hence, be sure to include these must-see sights and activities on your schedule for an amazing Italian journey in 2023.

Recommendations For Cultural Events And Festivals in Tuscany

Tuscany is renowned for its art, culture, and cuisine in addition to the numerous festivals and events that are held there all year long.

Everyone may find something to enjoy in Tuscany, regardless of their interests in music, art, gastronomy, or history. These are some of the most notable cultural occasions and celebrations to attend in Italy in 2023:

- **The Siena Palio**

Two times a year, the city of Siena hosts the Palio di Siena, a storied horse race. For everyone visiting Tuscany, the event is a must-see because it is so steeped in tradition.

The city comes alive with music, cuisine, and festivities in the days preceding the marathon, which takes place in the Piazza del Campo.

- **The Festival of Puccini**

The Giacomo Puccini Festival honors the composer's life and body of work. Every summer, the city of Lucca has a festival that includes opera performances and other cultural activities.

- **The Festival del Vino Chianti**

The world-famous wine produced in the area is celebrated at the Chianti Wine Festival. Visitors can try a wide range of wines from nearby wineries at the festival, which is held in the city of Greve in Chianti. They can also partake in food and entertainment.

- **The San Ranieri Luminara**

Every June, the city of Pisa has a festival called the Luminara di San Ranieri. Thousands of candles are used to brighten the streets and structures as part of the event, which honors the city's patron saint.

- **The Fiorentino Maggio Musicale**

Every year in Florence, there is a music festival called Maggio Musicale Fiorentino. A wide range of music, from classical to contemporary, is performed at the festival, which draws some of the top artists and performers in the world.

Twice a year, the city of Arezzo hosts the Giostra del Saracino, a medieval jousting competition. Anybody interested in medieval history must attend the tournament, which honors the city's heritage and history.

In summary, Tuscany hosts a wide range of cultural occasions and festivals that are likely to please any traveler. There is something for everyone in Tuscany, from traditional horse racing to music events and wine tastings. To fully experience Italian culture in 2023, be sure to attend these major festivals and events.

PART VI

EXPLORING TUSCANY'S OUTDOORS

The gorgeous scenery, undulating hills, and breathtaking countryside of Tuscany are well recognized. Visitors can engage in a range of outdoor activities in the area, including horseback riding, cycling, hot air balloon tours, and hiking. These are a few of the best outdoor pursuits and locations to visit in 2023 Italy:

- **The countryside of Tuscany**

For each traveler to Tuscany, the countryside is a must-see location. The natural splendor of the area is truly magnificent, from the vineyards of Montepulciano to the undulating hills of

Chianti. Tourists can take in the breathtaking views and breathe in the fresh air while exploring the area on foot, on bicycles, or even in a hot air balloon.

- **The Apennines hiking**

At Tuscany's eastern border are the Apennine Mountains, which are home to some of Italy's top hiking trails. The trails offer hikers breathtaking vistas of the surrounding countryside as they wind through forests and along mountain streams.

Among the top hiking destinations in the area are Mount Amiata and the Parco Nazionale delle Foreste Casentinesi.

- **The Coast of Maremma**

Visitors get the opportunity to take in Tuscany's stunning shoreline on the Maremma Coast. Visitors can swim and sunbathe in the Tyrrhenian Sea's crystal-clear waters and tour the area's environmental preserves and wildlife parks.

- **Italian cycling**

In Tuscany, cycling is a common pastime with several beautiful routes to choose from. Guests have the option of taking a guided tour that makes stops at nearby vineyards and farms, renting a bike to explore the area on their own, or both.

Cycling enthusiasts enjoy the network of unpaved country roads known as the Strade Bianche, or "white roads," which wind across the area's hills.

- **Equine riding**

The Tuscan landscape may be explored on horseback, and the area is home to a large number of stables and riding schools that provide guided tours.

Riders can experience the breathtaking environment from a different vantage point as they travel through vineyards, woodlands, and along the shore.

Tourists can enjoy a wide variety of outdoor activities and places in Tuscany. There is something for everyone in Tuscany's natural splendor, from hiking and cycling to horseback riding and hot air balloon tours. Thus, be sure to include these outdoor activities and locations in your 2023 adventure itinerary in Italy.

Tips For Getting The Most Out Of Tuscany's Outdoor Activities:

- **Think ahead.**

Planning is essential before engaging in any outdoor activity in Tuscany. Research the route or place you intend to travel, check the weather forecast, and make sure you are dressed appropriately and have the necessary equipment.

- **Employ a guide**

A guide should always be hired if you are unfamiliar with the area. Local tour operators can provide you with insider information about the area, show you undiscovered attractions that you would miss on your own, and assure your safety on strenuous treks and bike trips.

- **Take a trip off-season**

Peak season in Tuscany can be congested with visitors, which might ruin the outdoor experience. Think of going during the off-season when there are fewer tourists, milder temperatures, and more chances to peacefully take in the natural beauty of the area.

- **Try some of the local fares**

A highlight of any outdoor activity can be trying the local food and wine because Tuscany is known for its cuisine. For a sample of Tuscany's delectable cuisine, pack a picnic with local cheeses, meats, and bread, or arrange to visit a nearby vineyard or restaurant.

- **Be mindful of your surroundings.**

It's crucial to respect nature when exploring Tuscany's outdoor areas. Keep to established trails, pack away your waste, and try not to disturb wildlife or harm the environment.

- **Take breaks to admire the view.**

Slowing down can help you fully enjoy Tuscany's natural splendor. Take breaks, pause to snap pictures, and just soak in the wonderful view. Avoid the need to rush through your outdoor activity to see everything; instead, absorb the moment.

You may enjoy Tuscany's outdoors to the fullest extent by paying attention to these insider recommendations. Planning carefully, showing consideration for others, and savoring the moment can assure an amazing journey in the heart of Italy, whether you choose to hike in the Apennines or cycle through the countryside.

PART VII

TUSCANY LODGING OPTIONS

Here is a guide on where to stay in Tuscany, which provides a wide range of lodgings, from rural farmhouses and villas to opulent hotels and spas:

- **Agriturismos**

Farmhouses or other rural estates that have been transformed into lodging are known as agriturismos; they provide guests with an authentically rustic experience in Tuscany and frequently provide on-site activities like wine tastings or cookery classes.

- **Villas**

For those looking for seclusion and luxury, villas are a popular option. These roomy houses frequently have gardens, pools, and breathtaking views of the nearby countryside.

- **Hotels**

Tuscany offers a variety of lodging options, from boutique hotels to opulent resorts, many of which are built in old structures or have breathtaking views of the area's rolling hills and vineyards.

- **Overnight accommodations**

For those looking for a more personal experience, bed, and breakfasts are a pleasant and economical choice; these establishments provide a warm welcome and frequently provide a home-cooked breakfast each morning.

- **Glamping**

Glamping, which offers distinctive lodgings like yurts, tents, and treehouses, is a choice for individuals who want to enjoy the outdoors without sacrificing comfort.

- **Apartments**

Flats range from basic studios to magnificent penthouses, making renting one a fantastic choice for travelers who need more room or intend to stay in one location for an extended amount of time.

Consider the location - do you want to be in a big city or a peaceful rural area? Look for accommodations that offer features you'll appreciate, like a pool or on-site restaurant. And be sure to book early, especially during high season, to ensure availability.

Tuscany has a wide range of lodging options, so no matter whether you're looking for rustic charm or opulent comfort, you can find a place to stay that will make your trip to Tuscany unforgettable.

Tips For Selecting The Ideal Lodging In Tuscany

With so many lodging options available, if you're planning a trip to Tuscany, it can be difficult to choose the best one. Here are some insider suggestions to make the process easier:

- **Determine your budget**

Determine how much you're prepared to pay before you start looking, and bear in mind that rates might vary dramatically depending on the region and time of year. Tuscany provides a wide range of lodging alternatives, from affordable to luxurious.

- **Choose your location:**

Decide the locations you want to see and focus your search appropriately. For example, if you want to be close to Florence, check for lodgings in or around the city. Tuscany is a huge region with a variety of towns and cities to explore.

- **Research your options:**

Read reviews from previous visitors, look at images and descriptions of the properties to get a sense of what each one offers, and do some research on the various sorts of lodgings available in the area once you've settled on your budget and location.

- **Think about the amenities**

Search for properties that offer the amenities you desire to guarantee a pleasant and happy stay. Consider what amenities are important to you, such as a pool, restaurant, or spa.

- **See whether it's available**

Make sure to verify the availability of your desired accommodations well in advance and book early to prevent disappointment. Tuscany is a popular destination, especially during peak vacation season.

- **Contact the manager or owner**

Don't hesitate to contact the owner or manager of the property if you have any queries or concerns; they can offer more details and assist you in making an informed choice.

Tuscany boasts a wide choice of lodgings to suit every taste and budget, whether you're searching for a rural farmhouse or a sumptuous villa.

By using these insider suggestions, you can locate the ideal location to stay in Tuscany and make the most of your Italian experience.

PART VIII

PLANNING YOUR TUSCANY TRIP

It might be difficult to plan a trip to Tuscany, but with little planning, you can make the most of your time there. Here are some insider hints to assist you in organizing your trip to Tuscany:

- **Select the ideal time to visit**

Although Tuscany may be visited all year long, the ideal time to go will depend on your preferences. The busiest and most expensive season is summer, but it also has the greatest weather and the widest variety of outdoor activities.

The seasons of spring and fall are less congested, have pleasant temperatures, and have stunning foliage. The quietest time of year is winter, but many restaurants and attractions can be closed.

- **Make a plan for your travels**

There are numerous villages and cities to discover throughout Tuscany, each with its character. Decide the places you wish to see and then create an itinerary for them.

Remember that the winding roads and mountainous landscape of Tuscany can cause travel times to be longer than anticipated.

- **Think about your alternatives for getting there:**

The ideal way to see Tuscany is by automobile because it gives you the greatest flexibility and enables you to visit smaller towns and rural areas. Public transit choices include trains and buses if you don't want to drive. Remember that public transit may not be readily available in rural locations.

- **Reserve lodging in advance**

The lodgings in Tuscany can get booked up quickly, especially during the busiest travel times. To guarantee availability and to take advantage of early bird savings, make your hotel reservations in advance.

- **Arrange your excursions and sights**

From visiting museums and art galleries to wine tasting and hiking, Tuscany boasts a wide range of attractions and activities.

To make the most of your stay in the area, do your research and prepare a plan for your activities in advance.

- **Preparing properly**

Pack layers because the temperature in Tuscany might fluctuate throughout the day. You must wear comfortable shoes, especially if you intend to trek or visit the countryside. For outdoor activities, don't forget to bring sunscreen, a hat, and insect repellent.

You can make the most of everything Tuscany has to offer by planning a memorable trip with these insider suggestions.

Tuscany is a place that should be on every traveler's bucket list because of its fascinating history, vibrant culture, and magnificent scenery.

Outline Of The Major Celebrations And Events That Take Place In Tuscany Each Year

Tuscany is an area renowned for its rich cultural legacy, and there are many festivals and events held there throughout the year to honor its history, art, music, food, and wine.

The following are some of the most popular festivals and events in Tuscany that you can schedule to attend while there:

- **Carnival of Viareggio:**

This carnival, which takes place in February, is one of the biggest in Italy and boasts elaborate papier-mâché floats and costumes that march along the town's seashore.

- **Fiorentino Musicale Society**

This music festival, which takes place in Florence from May to June, presents a range of performances, such as ballet, opera, and classical music.

- **Italian Palio**

Two times a year, on July 2nd and August 16th, the city of Siena hosts this illustrious horse race. Ten horses and riders representing various communities compete in the race, which is hotly contested.

- **Storico Calcio**

This unusual sport, which mixes aspects of wrestling, rugby, and soccer, is played in Florence every June. The famous Piazza Santa Croce hosts a competition between teams from various districts.

- **Summer Festival in Lucca**

The worldwide performers performing at this music festival, which takes place in Lucca in July, come from a variety of musical genres, including jazz, rock, and pop.

- **Festival of Chianti Classico Wine**

This event honors the region's well-known Chianti wine and is held in September. It is held in Greve in Chianti and offers wine tastings, food vendors, and cultural activities.

- **Festival of truffles**

This event honors the truffle, a renowned component in Tuscan cuisine, and is held in November. It includes truffle hunting, tastings, and cookery demonstrations and is held in San Miniato.

- **San Ranieri's Candle**

Thousands of candles are lit during this celebration in Pisa each June, illuminating the city's iconic bridges and landmarks.

- **Markets for Christmas:**

Many villages and communities in Tuscany host traditional Christmas markets that sell food, crafts, and gifts during the holiday season.

These are just a few of the numerous celebrations and occasions that happen all around Tuscany every year. You can have an unforgettable experience of the area's culture and traditions by organizing your trip around one of these occasions.

EXPENSIVE BLUNDERS: ITALY TRAVEL DOS AND DON'TS

One of the most exciting aspects of any holiday is learning how to navigate a new place. Nothing is more satisfying than finding new landscapes and obscure places to explore.

Yet recently, one couple learned the disadvantage of forging ahead in new routes when they became stopped on a mountain pass after following Google maps. They ultimately needed to be saved by the neighborhood emergency services.

Due to this, the Sardinian village famous for its untamed terrain and meandering roads took precautions and put up signs along roads cautioning visitors not to use Google Maps. In only the last two years, there have been 144 rescue calls in the area.

It takes us to our first piece of advice.

1. Don't depend on your smartphone for directions (all the time)

Take no chances by relying just on your phone.
Take no chances by relying just on your phone.

Everyone's best travel companions are smartphones and user-friendly maps. Finding restaurants, coffee shops, and attractions has never been simpler thanks to simple-to-follow directions and the flexibility to filter results based on what you're looking for. However, you should occasionally check your surroundings or you can find yourself becoming lost.

It's one thing to walk through a forest to go to a shop, but this becomes extremely crucial if you plan to drive while on your trip because some of the most popular maps frequently fail to account for impassable paths.

Take note of coasts, small roads, and pedestrianized streets, and make sure you are familiar with your route (and not just the one on your smartphone) before starting. Italy has numerous narrow paths and coastlines, and failing to take care of them can prove fatal.

2. Ensure that your train ticket is valid.
a railroad route in Umbria

If you neglect to validate your tickets, the controllers won't be patient with you.

The vast network of railroads and public transportation is one of Europe's biggest advantages, as most individuals who have traveled there would attest.

Trains are a great way to get around quickly since they provide you the chance to move between cities and take scenic day trips. However, navigating the system can occasionally feel a little intimidating, so why not choose ItaliaRail instead?

It offers customer service in English around the clock, shows the entire day's train timetable, and enables you to buy tickets for up to 20 people at once. The phrase "and the Lounge has the Terminator"

But, it's crucial to authenticate your ticket before boarding any regional or local train in Italy. You should be able to see a green and yellow machine at the station where you may insert your ticket to get the date and time stamped.

This guideline is simple to follow, but many tourists are unaware of it because there isn't much information about it on the railroads themselves, and the only place it is written is in tiny text (in Italian) on the back of your train ticket.

Anyone who forgets is responsible for paying a fee that can be as low as €50 if they pay the controller right away and as much as €100 to €200 if they contest the case or fail to pay right away. By this point, the controllers have heard every defense and are unaffected by it. As a result, trying to reason your way out of the fine is rarely successful.

See our guide to touring Italy by train for more information on getting from one city to another.

3. Watch out for the "daily specials" in southern Italy, pasta

The Italian dish orecchiette is from the Puglia region.

Even though we may have a bias, we at Walks are delighted to say that Italy is one of the best countries in the world for wonderful food. There is truly something for everyone with a variety of cheesy treats, pastries, vegetarian options, and more traditional regional specialties. Yet, one thing that guests should be mindful of when dining out is the menu pricing.

There's nothing better than a holiday to eat what you want. A fantastic suggestion is to make sure you price-check the menu (for drinks too!), avoid ordering anything marked as a special (which typically doesn't have prices specified), and avoid going to the large touristy eateries.

They will frequently be the priciest options available, and if the price isn't stated upfront you have to ask a server, it might be terrible. This applies to coffee shops as well, where travelers are frequently given unpleasant surprises for a straightforward cappuccino.

Check out our article on how to save money while eating out in Italy for more information on dining out.

4. Pack light

Throughout your vacation through Italy, you'll probably want to buy a few souvenirs!
Of course, this applies to practically any vacation; the objective is always to find methods to bring less and pack less. But this is especially true for vacations to Italy, where the streets are typically winding and old.

Restoration efforts for significant pathways and paths are ongoing because many of them have been damaged over time by the weight of wheeled luggage. So packing less will make your trip more fun as well as being good for the city.

Trust me, attempting to carry a 20-kg suitcase up the Spanish Steps is a Promethean effort.

However, there are several things you can do to reduce the weight of your luggage, such as using hotel amenities and washing your clothing while you're there. Your trip will be more about taking in the sights and sounds of the city unless you're planning a luxurious break.

Nonetheless, if you are considering a lavish getaway, you should look through our list of Rome's most fashionable hotels.

Not sure what to pack for your Italy trip? See our helpful packing guide.

5. Avoid dining establishments with wait staff outside

Spend some time strolling the streets to discover a quiet restaurant off the usual road. They exist in every city. Because there is so much to see and do, Italy has its fair share of tourist traps that afflict prominent locations and sites worldwide.

These venues will seem quite attractive from the outside, but they are actually designed to entice you in and then spit you out. But when you delve further, you'll see why.

Unwary tourists seeking an authentic Italian experience will find themselves faced with small portions and expensive menus. These are not only among the most costly places to dine, but they also frequently provide the least fascinating and least varied menu options.

You won't have any trouble finding typical Italian fares like lasagna and spaghetti since restaurants are eager to capitalize on tourists' "ideas" of Italy, but if you try to get sfogliatella or panforte, you rarely have any luck. Instead, do some study beforehand and find some more authentic (and affordable) locations.

Also, our blog is a terrific resource for advice on dining out in Rome, Venice, and Florence if you're serious about finding the best places to grab a snack.

6. Purchase your tickets beforehand.

Everyone desires a tranquil, stress-free vacation. Many tourists believe they can get last-minute tickets for popular sights and enter without waiting in line, but this rarely happens.

Strangely, being as organized as you can is the key to a stress-free journey. If you prepare as much as you can in advance, all you have to do is enjoy the fruits of your labors and not worry about the minutiae when you arrive.

While making travel arrangements to Italy, it's important to keep in mind that you should buy tickets for all of the attractions you wish to visit well in advance. It could be a matter of weeks or even months.

While most people think to buy tickets for larger attractions like the Vatican, it's also a good idea to purchase them for smaller sites that can also sell out far in advance or, for places like the Borghese Gallery (pictured), it's worth taking a tour that includes tickets to get the most of your visit.

In Italy, you typically have to reserve tickets for a specified date and time. Instead of letting this ruin the spontaneity of your trip, it frequently makes it more laid back.

You'll be able to schedule in "free time" for whatever you choose once you know when you'll be busy seeing sights, whether that's walking through side streets and piazzas and happening onto secret spots or looking for the best gelato. While you'll be able to keep track of how much you've spent on attractions, which are typically the most expensive aspect of a vacation, buying everything in advance can also help you save money. In this manner, you'll simply need to set aside money for extras.

Going to Milan? Check out our buying advice for the coveted Last Supper tickets.

7. Bring some cash and a card.

A few euros are rattling in your pocket. They can only do one thing! This one has caused some debate in travel advice sections, with some arguing that using a card alone is sufficient.

The main issue with this is that you wouldn't have any other options if card payments weren't accepted or the machine broke down. It's best to be safe than sorry even though the majority of locations in Italy will have ATMs and card readers.

Dividing up your payment methods (and where you carry them) is another effective loss and theft prevention measure. Take out a predetermined sum of money and utilize it as a reserve (keeping track of the amount). In the worst-case scenario, you can put it back in your account after your vacation if you haven't used it.

A more real experience shouldn't be missed just because you didn't want to take cash around. While the more touristy restaurants and shops typically have credit machines, more traditional locations, such as stalls, markets, and tiny restaurants, may not. The same holds if you venture outside of Italy's well-known tourist areas.

THE BEST OF TUSCANY AND BEYOND: Wonderful Trips from Florence.

Get the top day trips from Florence here.

This guide covers everything from quaint medieval hilltop towns and rolling hills to coastal getaways and bustling cities!

It's a dream to carefully explore Florence, a gorgeous Renaissance city. Although we could easily devote weeks to studying its art, history, and culture, we understand that many tourists travel to Italy on shorter vacations to maximize their time and see as much as they can.

Florence is a prime location for this kind of journey.

Many of Tuscany's most famous attractions are accessible in less than an hour by car, and the high-speed rail that departs from the city center connects you to a number of the country's most stunning and sought-after cities and seaside locations.

Together with our suggestions for the top excursions, you'll discover a personal selection of our favorite day trips from Florence in this guide, along with all the details you need to go there on your own.

1. STEP BACK IN TIME IN SIENA

A visit to Siena is like traveling through time.

It served as Italy's main center for trade and finance during the 12th and 13th centuries. As the Medicis started their struggle for control in the 14th century, Florence gained this appellation.

During the Black Plague, Siena fell into a downward spiral marked by power battles between merchants and aristocrats, economic stagnation, and dictatorial rule under French and Spanish invasions, which culminated in surrender to the Spanish in 1555.

Despite all, Siena nonetheless managed to retain its charm and authenticity, with its red-brick structures and narrow, winding medieval lanes remaining untouched.

In our opinion, Siena requires more than one day to truly appreciate (we stayed there for three full days a few months ago), but the highlights may be seen in a full day of sightseeing.

Some of the items to not miss are listed below:

Piazza del Campo (maps) | This piazza, with its restaurants, boutiques, and bars lining the shell-shaped square, is the hub of Siena life. Tourists attempting to capture the splendor of the city coexist with locals going about their daily lives or relaxing on any given day. Jacopo della Quercia's Fonte Gaia is located in the center of the square.

If you're willing to climb the 400 steps to the top of the Torre del Mangia, which is a part of the plaza, you can get a different perspective on Siena. We advise purchasing your ticket as soon as you arrive to guarantee you can acquire a slot at a convenient time. Your ticket will grant you 30 minutes of viewing time.

Duomo di Siena (maps) | Although Florence's Duomo is unquestionably stunning, Siena's offers some fierce competition with its marble exterior created by Giovanni Pisano, Pinturicchio's paintings, and statues by Michelangelo, Donatello, and Bernini. Unmissable!

The oldest hospital in Europe, Santa Maria della Scala (maps), is now a museum housing murals, artifacts, and collections from Tuscany's past.

Do It On Your Own
51 kilometers (km) south of Florence is Siena, which is very accessible by public transportation.

The Santa Maria Novella train station in Florence has hourly direct trains to Siena (maps). A single ticket costs $9.80 and the trip takes about 1.5 hours. Please be advised that Siena's railway station is in the city's new section and that it will take 20 minutes to walk there from there.

You could also board Bus 131R, which leaves from Florence's bus terminal. It takes 80 minutes, which is a little less time than the train, but make sure you board the rapid bus rather than the ordinary, which has a slightly longer travel time. The bus schedule is available here.

The entire Siena historic center is a ZTL (zona a traffico limitato), thus driving there is not recommended, even if it makes for a very scenic trip. If you're driving or need a car for whatever reason, you'll need to park outside the ancient city walls and enter on foot.

Go On A Tour

While getting to Siena by public transportation is fairly several excellent tours departing frtoursrtfrom Florence if you'd prefer to travel extensively, delve deeper into the city's history, and visit multiple well-known locations in the surrounding Tuscan countryside. These include:

Get a taste of the Tuscan countryside on this all-day excursion from Florence to Siena and San Gimignano, which includes lunch at a family-owned vineyard, matched with regional wines, and a chance to see the medieval hill town of San Gimignano. Go here to learn more.

Day trip to Siena, San Gimignano, and Monteriggioni | This highly popular full-day tour follows a similar itinerary to the one above, but instead of lunch, there is a wine tasting (it has thousands of outstanding reviews). Also, it is longer, giving you more time to explore San Gimignano and Siena. Go here to learn more.

Tuscany Day Tour | Our last top-rated tour suggestion includes a lunch stop and a wine tasting in the Chianti Hills, as well as a guided tour of Siena, free time in San Gimignano, the opportunity to see the Leaning Tower of Pisa.

To make the most of your time, you can also choose to travel alone to Siena and then take a guided tour of the city's top attractions; this option includes a two-hour walking tour and skip-the-line Duomo tickets.

2. FIESOLE IS THE PLACE TO SEE

A picture-perfect hilltop village by the name of Fiesole is located on the hills five miles northeast of Florence. It has been owned by the Etruscans, Romans, and then Florentines throughout the centuries, becoming a residence for the city's nobility in the fourteenth century.

It served as the setting for Boccaccio's Decameron, the site where Galileo and Milton observed the sky and the location where Leonardo da Vinci tested his hypothesis of flight.

Importantly, the Renaissance-style village also offers up a spectacular and expansive view of the area below, including lush rolling hills, red roofs atop white-washed buildings, rows and rows of cypress trees, and finally the lovely Florence herself, for visitors seeking a break from the busy streets and city life.

The Convent San Francesco offers the best view of the area, and history buffs shouldn't miss the Etruscan-Roman Archeological Area (maps), which is home to the remains of the ancient Etruscan town walls, a Roman Theatre, and a temple. Inside, you'll find art collections from Egypt, China, and Florence.

Do It On Your Own

Fiesole is the ideal day trip from Florence because it is very accessible and can be accessed by bus in only 20 minutes. From San Marco Square or Santa Maria Novella train station, take Bus Route 7 to the "Stazione Nazionale â€" Largo F.lli Alinari" stop. Each way tickets cost 1.50 and can be purchased in advance or onboard.

Alternatively, it's a quick 25-minute journey if you have a car. Both this Piazza del Mercato and the nearby archeological area have plenty of parking.

You can also walk to Fiesole if you don't mind getting a little workout. A reasonably healthy person should be able to reach Fiesole from Florence's center in around 1.5 hours if they start along Via

Boccaccio and travel via the scenic Via Vecchia Fiesolana. Instead of following a freeway, there is an established hiking trail!

Go On A Tour

Consider taking this guided Vespa tour, which starts with a quick drive around Florence's top attractions before heading out into the countryside for a tour of Fiesole, if you're seeking a more distinctive approach to experiencing Fiesole. Go here to learn more.

Alternatively, this four-hour e-bike tour, which is led by a very knowledgeable guide, covers everything you need to see in Fiesole (along with a farm visit). The only drawback is that you will still need to make your way to Fiesole to start it.

3. LOOK AT THE PISA TOWER

Pisa probably doesn't need an introduction; it is home to the most famous tower in the entire world.

And while you could easily spend a few days in this surprisingly charming city,

Pisa makes for a wonderful day trip because of its proximity to Florence and the fact that its most famous attractions are concentrated in one breathtakingly magnificent area, the Campo Dei Miracoli.

While traveling alone, be sure to leave early to soak in the tower's views before the masses show up. Next, take your time touring the magnificent Duomo, the Battistero di San Giovanni, and the Camposanto Monumentale.

Please be aware that each of these monuments has a little convoluted booking process; you can find complete instructions on how to book and costs here, or you may book your skip-the-line tickets here.

We've produced several guides to the city, including this in-depth essay on seeing the Leaning Tower and the top things to do in Pisa, so we strongly suggest reading them before making travel arrangements.

Do It On Your Own

Pisa is only a little more than an hour's drive from Florence, but like most Italian cities, many of its main streets are no-car zones. If you plan to arrive by car, we advise parking at Via Pietrasantina (maps) and traveling to the Campo dei Miracoli by commuter bus. Parking is free, and each ride on the bus only costs one euro.

With many departures from Santa Maria Novella Station every hour (ranging in duration from 50 minutes to 2.5 hours, so confirm before purchasing), taking the train is probably a better alternative. Each way tickets cost 8.90 euros.

Go On A Tour

This well-liked six-hour option, which includes round-trip transportation, a guided tour of Pisa and Campo dei Miracoli, as well as admission passes to the Duomo and the Leaning Tower, is our suggestion for the finest Florence to Pisa tour. Go here to learn more.

If you don't want to climb the tower, think about taking this well-regarded shorter tour.

As an alternative, think about taking this Tuscany Day Tour if you want to visit Pisa and another well-known Tuscan destination. Although it is a lengthy tour, it is a viable alternative for visitors who have a limited amount of time in this region of Italy.

It includes lunch and a wine tasting in the Chianti Hills, a guided tour of Siena, free time in San Gimignano, the opportunity to see the Leaning Tower of Pisa, and a guided tour of Siena. Go here to learn more.

This trip should be reserved if you're willing to travel independently to Pisa but would want to join once you get there to see the city and Campo dei Miracoli.

4. GO TO SAN GIMIGNANO'S HILLTOP TOWN

The walled medieval village of San Gimignano, which was named a UNESCO

World Heritage Site in 1990, offers much of what makes Tuscany unique in one ideal, little, Instagrammable parcel.

Its hilltop location offers expansive views of lush valleys, cypress trees, and verdant vineyards, and its historic streets are a labyrinth of hidden churches and quintessential Tuscan charm. The city is known as the "Manhattan of the Middle Ages" for its numerous red-brick medieval towers, of which thirteen still stand today.

Due to its small size, San Gimignano may be visited in a single day from Florence, either on its own or in conjunction with some of the other charming small towns nearby.

There is no set itinerary required when visiting, although certain attractions are worth seeing:

Take a stroll up this bustling, yet narrow, street to find the best shopping. Via San Matteo (maps). Great leather products, trinkets, and regional things are available.

The only tower in San Gimignano's famed Piazza del Duomo that is accessible to the general public is Torre Grossa. Although it is 54 meters high and gives breathtaking views of the Tuscan countryside, the steep 218 stairs are not simple.

Visit the markets | If you plan your trip wisely, you should make a point of visiting the local markets, which are a great introduction to Italian culture. On Thursday, the focus is on crafts and local food vendors; on Saturday, it's fresh produce.

Avoid skipping the Duomo (maps) | From the exterior, the Duomo Collegiata di Santa Maria Assunta appears to be a very unassuming structure. But, as you enter, you will find a stunning collection of the best-preserved frescoes that date back to the 1300s and are still as vibrant as the day they were painted.

Do It On Your Own

The quickest and most convenient method to get to San Gimignano is by vehicle, which takes around an hour. Although parking is not permitted inside the historic district, there are numerous modest parking lots outside the fortifications. We advise coming here.

You must take a bus or train bound for Siena (additional information can be found in the Siena section) and switch to Bus 130 at Poggibonsi for the direct route to San Gimignano to reach the town via public transportation.

Regular bus service runs between Florence and Poggibonsi, with a 20-minute travel time, and between Poggibonsi and San Gimignano.

Go On A Tour

San Gimignano isn't the sole subject of any trip, although some highly well-liked itineraries depart from Florence and include it along with other well-known Tuscan locations:

Day trip to San Gimignano and Volterra with Food and Wine | Start the day in San Gimignano with a wine sampling, then travel to a nearby winery for lunch before finishing the day in Volterra.

Since there are only 4 people allowed, you'll have plenty of time to visit the sites you wish. Go here to learn more.

Day Tour to Siena, San Gimignano, and Chianti with Lunch | During this full-day tour, you have the option of taking a guided tour or exploring Siena and San Gimignano on your own. includes a classic Tuscan meal with wine pairing in the Chianti Hills. Go here to learn more.

Tour of Siena, San Gimignano, and Monteriggioni in One Day | On this extremely well-liked tour, you have about 8 hours to explore all three locations.

While Siena is guided, San Gimignano is yours to explore at your leisure. consists of a Chianti wine sampling as well! Learn more here.

While we believe that the Siena, Pisa, and San Gimignano tour may be cramming in a bit too much, it is tremendously well-liked and ranked, making it an excellent choice if you're short on time and want to see as much as you can. Go here to learn more.

5. BOLOGNA: WALK THE PORTICOES

We may be a little prejudiced because we have already been to Bologna twice (once for four glorious spring days and once for a week-long summer language school), but in all seriousness, this city is stunning.

Its university, the oldest continuously operating one in the world, contributes to the city's strong student life. It is home to endless porticoes and old family towers, a thriving food scene, great old buildings, and even grander squares.

We loved it and recorded a podcast episode about it.

Thus, this is a great option if you're searching for a day trip from Florence to what we consider to be one of the best towns in Italy, even though we sincerely believe that Bologna is a city that needs to be explored a little slowly.

Not-to-be-missed sights and activities include:

The Portico di San Luca leads to the magnificent Basilica di San Luca and is the longest-covered walkway in the world (it was previously a pilgrimage route).

Basilica di San Petronio | This church's construction never ended, despite starting in 1390, according to a rumor that the Pope didn't want it to be larger than Rome's. With its facade of pink and white marble, it is still stunning.

Eat tagliatelle al ragù | After you realize that spaghetti bolognese doesn't exist, you'll be delighting in Bologna's famous dish if you're a meat eater.

Climb the entire 498 steps of the Asinelli Tower. We assure you that the view is well worth it.

Visit the Teatro Anatomico | Bologna is as historically significant as its home to the oldest university in the world might suggest. The exquisitely elaborate anatomical theater is one location within that should not be missed.

Check to see if you can spot any hidden canals while you're wandering. Bologna's waterways are obscured by buildings, unlike Venice. Visit Via Piella (maps) and look through the windows to find these surprising locations.

Do It On Your Own
Using public transportation, specifically the standard intercity train that runs

between Santa Maria Novella and Bologna Centrale in approximately 40 minutes, is the simplest method to go to Bologna on your own. Tickets start at 12 euros per person; see our guide for important advice on Italian train travel.

Go On A Tour

As there are no special tours that take you back and forth between the two cities, we advise anyone interested in visiting on a day trip to take the train, then take a guided tour once they are in Bologna. These are two great choices:

Bologna Walking Tour | This well-liked, highly regarded, and reasonably priced two-hour walking tour of Bologna takes in the city's major attractions and serves as a wonderful introduction. Go here to learn more.

Bologna Food Tour | For those who prefer to learn about a new city through its cuisine, this 4.5-hour guided trip is perfect. includes visits to six historic stores and eateries where visitors may sample regional delicacies like tortellini, ragu, Parmigiano Reggiano, Aceto Balsamico di Modena, mortadella, and wine. Go here to learn more.

6. TO THE CHIANTI HILLS FOR A RESCUE

The Chianti Hills, a picturesque region with olive groves and oak and chestnut woods between Florence and Siena, are well-known for their wines.

The fact that one of the most well-liked days outings involves seeing the numerous vineyards and wineries that have been making these wines for more than 700 years should not come as a surprise.

In addition to the wine excursions, you can visit the following villages:

Greve (maps) | Greve is a little medieval town 30 kilometers from Florence that is well-known for its triangular-shaped square, which has long been the site of a delightful Saturday market. The Chianti Expo is also held there, where local wineries exhibit their products.

Radda is a typical Chianti hilltop village with plenty of ancient charm (maps). Wine has been made in the nearby countryside for more than a thousand years!

Castellina is a popular tourist site in the Chianti region and is a little larger than Radda. Don't overlook the magnificent stronghold that towers over the town and is home to the Museo Archeologico del Chianti Senese, which highlights the Etruscan origins of the Chianti.

Do It On Your Own

As one might anticipate, getting to the Chianti Hills is difficult with public transportation, so if you want to fully explore the area, you'll need your rental car. Just be sure to appoint a designated driver first!

This article offers suggestions for the top wineries to visit along with a terrific Chianti wine path to follow.

Go On A Tour

Although individuals who own cars may reach the area, we advise booking a tour of the Chianti Hills if your group's main goal is for everyone to taste the wines.

Chianti Afternoon Wine Tour | This tour takes you around the Tuscan countryside for two tastings and to learn the winemaker's secrets. Your guide is a wine specialist. Go here to learn more.

This small-soup experience is a great substitute that has received excellent ratings everywhere.

Chianti Wine Tasting Day Tour with Food | This excursion is another for Chianti connoisseurs and has received a great deal of praise. Take a tour of a guided wine cellar, a wine tasting (matched with local cheeses and meats), and some free time to explore a medieval village. Go here to learn more.

7. WALK AROUND LUCCA'S WALLED CITY

Little Lucca doesn't attract millions of tourists every summer with famous photo spots, world-class museums, or a history replete with illustrious Renaissance figures, unlike its neighbors to the south and the north.

But it's not relevant.

You can immediately relax in this tiny walled city. You can enjoy the cultured way of life and look for those little pleasures while riding your bicycle around historic walls, stopping for a mid-morning latte, and meandering down cobblestone streets.

It has a lot more going on than one might think, including being the unexpected location of both one of Italy's top summer music festivals and Europe's largest comic book convention.

An old northern Italian city with all its distinguishing features of medieval towers, palazzos, and piazzas, the allure of regional cuisine, artisans, and romance is a very remarkable location.

We strongly advise reading our in-depth guide to the top things to do in Lucca before making travel arrangements.

But be sure to pay attention to the following:

Follow the City Walls | Because Lucca is known as the "walled city," any trip there should involve a stroll or a ride around the top of their outer perimeter for stunning views of both the historic district and the surrounding countryside. An excellent first action after arrival.

Climb Torre Guigini (maps) | many towers in Italy can be scaled, but we believe this is the only one that has trees sprouting from the top.

Piazza dell'Anfiteatro (maps) | This city's main square is an architectural wonder that is a combination of an antique amphitheater and a piazza.

There are numerous crowded eateries and cafes where you can have a drink or lunch outside within its arcaded walls. There are artisanal goods or vegetable kiosks put up during the day, and at night there is a delightful social environment to match the unusual surroundings.

On two wheels, like the natives, is the finest way to see the city! Also, it implies that you can travel farther, which is perfect for a day excursion. In our Lucca guide, you can discover complete information about renting a bike as well as other things to do.

Do It On Your Own

Every hour, trains depart from Santa Maria Novella and go to Lucca in an hour and fifteen minutes. Tickets cost nine dollars for each trip.

Instead, driving from Florence to Lucca takes one hour and ten minutes. Parking outside the city walls is advised. The majority of Lucca is a ZTL, which means that driving is prohibited and that parking can be very expensive. Consider Parcheggio Carducci (maps).

Go On A Tour

Your best option is to take the train from Florence and then sign up for a day trip if you want to concentrate all of your day's activities on Lucca.

For instance, this two-hour walking tour of the city's historic center gives you a fantastic introduction to the area while also giving you time to go at your own pace.

Our Pisa & Lucca day tour is a great alternative if you want to make the most of your sightseeing opportunities. It includes admission to the Pisa Duomo, guided tours of both Pisa and Lucca, and the opportunity to sample Buccellato, a typical Lucchese confection, at the conclusion! Go here to learn more.

Start your planning with our Lucca travel guide.

8. IDENTIFY THE PERFECT VAL D'ORCIA IN THE IMAGE

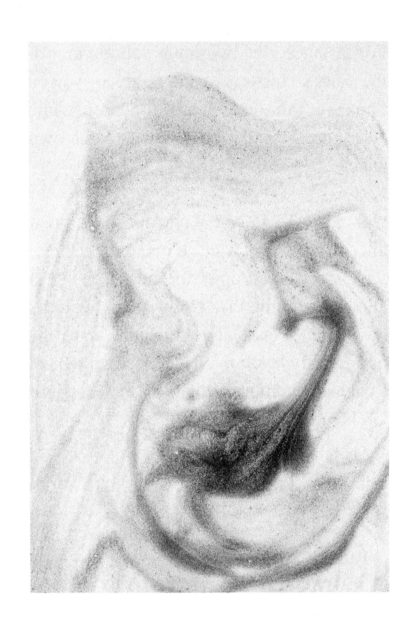

The breathtaking Val D'Orcia, a UNESCO Site of Exceptional Beauty, stretches between Siena and Grosseto. This picture may be what originally lured you to Tuscany.

It is a picture-postcard-perfect valley, lush with unending vineyards, olive groves, abandoned farmhouses, abbeys, and old castles.

The Val d'Orcia is a sizable region that might be slowly explored on a separate road trip, however notable locations to take into consideration are as follows:

The thermal springs at Bagni San Filippo are equally as stunning, although being less well-known than the insta-famous Terme di Saturnia. This is especially true given that they are surrounded by a forest.

In addition to serving as a rest stop for travelers heading to Rome in the Middle Ages, Buonconvento was also a significant commerce center.

San Quirico d'Orcia (maps) | The renowned copse of cypress trees, for which the valley is renowned, is located just outside of San Quirico d'Orcia. Golden hour is when the scene comes to life, despite being beautiful throughout the day. Spend some time exploring the town's streets, stopping for lunch, and stopping at the Collegiata of the Saints Quirico and Giulietta.

The typical Tuscan hilltop village of Montepulciano sits overlooking the Val d'Orcia and the Val di Chiana. Enjoy winding ancient alleyways, breathtaking views of the countryside, majestic cathedrals, museums, and the Piazza Grande.

It also happens to be the birthplace of one of our favorite Italian red wines, the Montepulciano.

Pienza (maps) is one of the biggest cities in the Val d'Orcia and was previously Pope Pius II's summer retreat. Nevertheless, it is arguably now more known as the location of the Netflix series Medici.

Do It On Your Own

You must rent a car to go to Val d'Orcia because it cannot be reached by public transportation. Driving through the Chianti Hills takes an hour and 50 minutes, but allow extra time because there are many locations to pause for photos.

Go On A Tour

We endorse this tour for cheese and wine tasting. It is a lengthy tour that lasts about twelve hours, but it has received a ton of positive feedback with visits to Pienza, Montepulciano, and a winery in Montalcino.

9. PURSUE THE CINQUE TERRE

The Cinque Terre, a UNESCO World Heritage Site of famed colorful coastal hamlet clusters that fall toward the waves in a perfect pastel patchwork, is a location to savor for its natural and man-made treasures rather than a place full of museums, ruins, or attractions.

It's about swimming in the salty sea and enjoying freshly fried local anchovies from a greasy paper cone, hiking alongside hand-selected ancient vines, stealing sunsets from picture-perfect vantage points, and filling every sense with the happiness that can only be experienced on an Italian sun escape.

We just spent a week seeing the five towns, and we firmly believe that given the challenges with over-tourism, this tiny

Italian destination is dealing with, they are more deserving of just a day trip.

They continue to be a well-liked fast stop on many itineraries, particularly on day trips from Florence. We advise day-trippers to concentrate on one or a few of the following to avoid spreading themselves too thin:

Monterosso beach for a few hours (maps) | Who says day trips from Florence have to involve tours and tower climbing? Sometimes all we want to do is kick off our shoes and spend the day at the beach, and Monterosso's is especially picturesque!

Walk

There are many hiking paths in Cinque Terre, but the "Blue Trail," which links Monterosso al Mare and Corniglia, is the most well-known.

Go to the seas

This day trip is the ideal way to get out of the city and get some peace on the seaside. For those who want an active tour, we suggest this speedboat tour of the Cinque Terre, which departs from La Spezia.

Try the regional specialties, which include Cinque Terre wine and greasy fried seafood served in paper cones (our favorite was in Riomaggiore).

Tour the Villages

While we are aware that it would be quite alluring to attempt to visit all five villages, we advise you to think about concentrating only on two or three.

Do It On Your Own

Whilst technically conceivable, we don't advise driving your car to the Cinque Terre villages for several reasons. Instead, travel to La Spezia in a car for 1.5 to 2.5 hours, park, and then take the train to the villages.

Although there are trains from Florence to La Spezia (from where you would need to change into the 5T Express Train), the direct alternative only departs every two hours, which could make returning a little challenging or result in a very long day.

Because of this, we advise taking a tour if you only have a day to explore Cinque Terre.

Go On A Tour

Day Excursion to Cinque Terre | Because of its flexibility, this full-day tour is one of the best-rated. You have the choice to trek and join the group for lunch, and it passes through all five villages. Go here to learn more.

Conversely, if you just want transportation without having to deal with the trains from Florence, this tour is also well-liked and is available at a comparable price point, but it excludes the option to add on lunch or go hiking as a group.

10. A TRIP TO VENICE, THE FLOATING TREASURE.

Italy's tourism behemoths include Florence and Venice, each of which requires weeks of exploration to fully comprehend their lengthy histories, the political, theological, and cultural movements they were influenced by, and the people who led them.

Understanding Venice's geography and its intricate canal system, which enabled the city to flourish, adds another layer of complexity to the subject.

And even though we firmly believe that this floating treasure chest of a city is well worth at least a few days of your Italian getaway (and day trips add to its over-tourism problem), we understand that for many, time is rather limited and cutting back on bases and taking short trips is more practical.

We have a specific article on 13 Great Things to Do in Venice, but if you decide to visit Venice for a day trip, we suggest including the following on your itinerary:

The Doge's Palace, a stunning structure with beautiful porticoes overlooking the river and decorated in pastel pink and white diamond tiles, served as the center of Venetian power (and the residence of the Doge) beginning around 810 AD. So make sure to plan and purchase your tickets.

The Bridges | Venice is a city of bridges, and you'll pass by a lot of them just by walking about. However, you should be sure to include Rialto Bridge, The Bridge of Sighs, and Ponte dell'Accademia on your trip.

Gondola Ride | Is there anything more authentically Venetian than a gondola ride across the city's canals? Not cheap, but probably at the top of many people's lists of things to do. Our guide on riding a gondola in Venice contains all the information you require.

St. Mark's Square | Perhaps Venice's most well-known attraction, a stroll across the plaza is a must-do during any trip. Consider going into the Basilica and climbing the campanile if you have time.

Consume Cicchetti | Every pub, restaurant, and cafe in this region serves up cicchetti, a dish akin to tapas. Nonetheless, we suggest visiting Al Squero or Cantine del Vino gi Schiavi.

Do It On Your Own

Although it is theoretically possible to drive to Venice, we don't advocate it for several reasons. Instead, use the high-speed train that runs between the two cities.

There are frequent departures throughout the day from Santa Maria Novella railway station, and the trip takes just over two and a half hours.

The cost of a ticket rises as you get closer to the departure date; same-day tickets cost 50 euros, while tickets purchased two weeks in advance cost 30 euros.

Here, you may check the costs and availability.

Go On A Tour

There aren't many tours online that offer this particular day excursion from Florence, but if you're interested in visiting Venice, think about signing up for this well-regarded, full-day trip that includes transportation and is self-paced with a guide around to offer suggestions.

11. TRAVEL THROUGH ROME

One of the world's most seductive and endearing towns, Italy's lively capital is a lovely blend of Roman ruins, eye-catching art, and dynamic street life.

Because there are so many things to do, we have already been twice and have barely scratched the surface (we have big intentions to go back for a two-week trip to dig under its skin).

Because of this, we actually wouldn't suggest that you visit as a day excursion, except for three important factors:

With a high-speed train, Florence is easily accessible.

If it's your first time visiting Italy and you're probably not going to return for a while, you should include this on your schedule.

The majority of the city's top attractions are concentrated in a relatively limited region.

If you were planning a day trip, we'd suggest the following:

The Colosseum (maps) | The Colosseum is arguably Rome's most well-known landmark. Take some time to stroll around the tunnels.

Roman Forum (maps) | The Forum, the city's principal square and the center of public life, was the beating heart of ancient Rome. The collection of streets, arches, temples, and towering columns provides a remarkable glimpse into life in this most signific Roman cis unicity years ago, even though some areas have been seriously damaged.

Climb Palatine Hill (maps) | Palatine Hill is a ruinous region that served as Rome's starting location, located across from the Colosseum.

You are rewarded with a fantastic city panorama, including the Colosseum, Roman Forum, and St. Peter's Basilica in the distance, after a brief ascent.

Visit St. Peter's Square (maps) | A journey to the Vatican is a requirement for every vacation to Rome. If you leave Florence early enough, you might have time to visit the Sistine Chapel and Basilica in addition to St. Peter's Square, especially if you pre-purchase a skip-the-line tickct.

Numerous other significant landmarks in the city, such as the Trevi Fountain, the

Spanish Steps, and, if you make an extra effort, the Pantheon, can be seen on the hour-long walk from the Forum (and its associated buildings) to the Vatican. Just keep in mind that you have a lot to fit in, so don't linger for too long!

Do It On Your Own
While you could drive from Florence to Rome, like with Venice, we wouldn't suggest it. There are too many tolls, excessive travel times, and pricey parking.

Instead, we advise taking the train, which runs frequently throughout the day from Florence's Santa Maria Novella station to Rome. The trip lasts roughly 1.5 hours, and tickets can be purchased for as little as $20 if purchased in advance (just make sure you board the fast train!). The cost per person will climb to about 50 euros if you book on the spot.

Go On A Tour

Your best option is to travel alone by rail and then join a guided tour of the city since we are unable to find a specific group that covers transportation from Florence to Rome.

Although you won't be able to find a tour that covers all the things we've listed above because the Vatican is officially in a different nation from the rest of Rome's attractions, we do recommend these two:

Colosseum, Roman Forum, and Palatine Hill | This wildly popular guided trip with a Roman history expert includes skip-the-line admission to all three major attractions. Go here to learn more.

Sistine Chapel, Basilica, and Vatican Museums: This outstanding and highly regarded three-hour trip includes the key Vatican sights and is accompanied by a knowledgeable guide.

contains fast-track entry as well, which is necessary if you want to cover the territory quickly. Go here to learn more.

USEFUL ADVICE FOR TRAVELING ALONE

Buses, railroads, and various driving excursions have all been used extensively as we have traversed Italy.

The challenge of living in Florence is that many areas of the city are off-limits to cars, and entering along the wrong way could result in a costly fine. This is also true when stopping down for a few days on a dedicated Tuscany road trip.

There are two alternatives to this.

Finding a place to stay with parking is the first step; most of them can be found in the Otranto neighborhood of the city, south of the river (but still within short walking distance to the main sights).

The second is to start in Florence and only rent a car once the actual road journey starts.

We rarely hire our road trip automobiles directly; instead, we evaluate prices and deals using two well-known rental aggregators. We work with two businesses: AutoEurope and RentalCars, both of which have provided us with fantastic service.

If you intend to rent a car while visiting Italy, we highly suggest reading our article, "Nine Important Car Rental Guidelines for Travelers," for general advice on how to cut costs on your car rental and steer clear of some typical vehicle rental blunders.

the journey by rail.

Italy has a wide-ranging, inexpensive, and reliable rail system. It's probably the greatest choice for any day trip you would want to take between cities.

Yet, there are a few peculiarities to be aware of before boarding your first train, all of which we've covered in this thorough overview of Italian train travel.

REASONS TO VISIT TUSCANY

There are many good reasons to travel to Tuscany!

The Stunning Views

Terraced landscapes and pastoral hills surround Tuscany, showcasing the elegant countryside as you travel through it. If you love the outdoors, just the commute itself will be worthwhile.

the location of Renaissance artists' births
The names of Leonardo da Vinci, Michelangelo, Raphael, Donatello, Caravaggio, and Jan van Eyck will make any art enthusiast swoon. Must I continue? The Renaissance movement was founded

in Tuscany, and these painters emerged from these same northern hills!

A Historical Relic from Italy

Go past centuries-old monuments and ancient city ruins for those who have a passion for historical information. If Italian history is what you're after, a vacation to Tuscany will provide lots of opportunities to witness it (tip: might be best to book yourself guided tours for the most historical context).

Important Landmarks

Some of Italy's most famous attractions, which are popular with both locals and tourists, are all across your journey. You will see them all, whether they are ancient cathedrals or medieval castles. San

Gimignano, Siena, and Pisa's masterpieces beckon to you!

Tuscany's Drink Your Way Through It
With some of the best local wines at your disposal, your trip can have a touch of scandal! You'll have the perfect amount of buzz to enjoy the breathtaking Italian landscape. Enjoy some delicious authentic Italian food while you're there!

Tuscany tours: Self-guided vs. guided
You're sure to be surrounded by the verdant Italian countryside whether you select guided or self-directed trips.

Personalized Trips

I strongly advise renting a car if you plan to spend more than a day in Florence so you can explore the Tuscan countryside on your own. This provides you the freedom to stop wherever you like on the spur of the moment and take in the beauty at your leisure. This is a guide to assist you in organizing your journey from Florence.

Assisted Tours

I advise you to think about guided tours if you're on a tight schedule or only have a short amount of time in the city. Your guide will lead the journey, so you can sit back, relax, and take in the breathtaking scenery of the Tuscan countryside without having to worry about a thing.

Access to all of the well-known attractions in Siena, San Gimignano, and Pisa, such as the Piazza del Campo, the Basilica of Sant'Agostino, the Piazza dei Miracoli, and others, is another benefit of taking a guided trip.

If you're leaning tow toward wardedurtowardve a look at the other Florence to Tuscany day trip tickets available here.

An Example Itinerary for a Guided Tour

The Tuscan region is too large to see everything in a single day. Moreover, rural Italy's public transportation system is not very well connected. The All Tuscany in a Day Tour, however, had a well-packed schedule that allowed me to make the most of my day.

As soon as you arrive at the agreed-upon meeting location, you will be picked up and taken to the heart of Tuscany.

Halt in Siena, a charming city renowned for its historical structures with Romanesque and Gothic influences. Visit a winery between Siena and San Gimignano, Piazza del Campo, and Piazza del Duomo.

Then, take a stroll into San Gimignano to take in the breathtaking scenery of this walled town that reveals a portion of medieval Europe.

Go through the charming streets of the renowned Chianti area to the city of Pisa, which is home to several hidden gems, including the Baptistery, the Cathedral, and, of course, the Leaning Tower of Pisa.

TOP THINGS TO DO IN TUSCANY

Tuscany, which still preserves the traditional Italian landscapes, is home to picturesque farmhouses, rolling vineyards and olive groves, ancient hilltowns, and alleyways lined with cypress trees.

You can only accomplish so much in a single day. While the "All Tuscany in a Day Tour" was enjoyable, if you have more time in Tuscany, there are a few other things you should do.

THE BEAUTIFUL CITY OF PISA
For The Lovers Of Photography

The Leaning Tower of Pisa is a must-see destination and one of the most famous structures in the world. The Campo dei Miracoli, the Romanesque Cathedral, the baptistery, the Camposanto, and other magnificent sites may all be found in Pisa.

ALPI APUANE, KISSED BY NATURE, Is For Hikers & Nature Lovers

Put on your walking shoes and visit the Alpi Apuane marble quarries in Northern Tuscany, which is regarded as something of a floral paradise.

Your strolling paths are lined with beautiful wildflowers, beech and chestnut trees, and more. The golden eagle, kestrels, sparrowhawks, and other local and foreign species can all be seen here.

PEOPLE WHO LOVE ART SHOULD VISIT THE UFFIZI GALLERY

Explore The Uffizi Gallery to take in the splendor of the Renaissance. containing the greatest collection of paintings from the Italian Renaissance in the world as well as one of Italy's finest art collections.

See the creations of renowned artists like Giotto, Da Vinci, Raffaello, Masaccio, Cimabue, and Da Vinci.

LA VERNA'S MONASTERIES
For The Lovers Of Heritage

Visit a mountaintop hideaway in La Verna, one of the most popular pilgrimage destinations in Tuscany. You'll have a fascinating time whether you're coming to pay your respects, check out the monks' quarters, or are just interested in what goes on at this popular pilgrimage.

GIGLIO'S ISLAND LIFESTYLE
Island Life For Beach Lovers

Giglio is a charming island off the coast of Tuscany that is ringed with beaches, stone villages, and picturesque citadels. Giglio is the perfect site to experience the good old island life in Tuscany because it is less developed and crowded than its neighboring island, Elba.

For foodies, Mugello offers truffle sampling
Even the Tuscans do not fully recognize the truffles, a gold mine that thrives in their backyard. Try this traditional Tuscan ingredient if you enjoy truffles (or truffle

oil). Visit Mugello or San Miniato without a doubt if you're looking for premium truffles.

WINE TASTING IN CHIANTI
For The Wine Lovers

No trip to Tuscany would be complete without a visit to the celebrated Tuscan vineyards. The long stretch of vineyards between Florence and Siena is home to some of Italy's finest appellations, so don't forget to pick yourself a bottle on your way back home.

Eu-Natural at Bagno Vignoni
FOR THE SPA LOVERS
Make your way to one of Tuscany's trendy spa towns, Bagno Vignoni, a tiny and vibrant village with a natural hot spring and a Medici-era pool. The pool is not

currently accessible, but the village is still lined with free outdoor sulfur pools for you to take a dip in.

BEST WAY TO TRAVEL FROM FLORENCE TO TUSCANY

It depends on what you hope to gain from the trip, but let me start by noting there is no correct response to this issue.

There are numerous public transit alternatives available in Florence, the city of Tuscany. Although most of Tuscany's towns and cities have public transit, the connectivity provided in the smaller towns like Chianti and San Gimignano is far less reliable.

Here are all the many routes you can take from Florence to travel throughout Tuscany.

Going from Florence to Tuscany - All your options listed

Mode of Travel Time Cost Best For
Car, 1 hour 20 minutes   from $9   per gallon .   Freedom to stop at leisure

Bus 2 hours   from €7.80 Economically feasible

Train 1 hour 30 minutes   from €6.80
Comfortable journeys
Organized Tour 12 - 14

Driving from Florence to Tuscany

Four wheels were created for Tuscany. Cruising along these frequently deserted country roads, which are banked like racetracks at every curve, is a thrill in and of itself. If you plan to drive yourself to

Tuscany, I'd suggest investing in a fantastic rental car; whether it's a Fiat 124 or a Fiat Spider convertible, you're sure to have fun either way.

The Florence airport is home to a large number of automobile rental companies. The ideal travel time would be an hour and a half from Florence to Siena or San Gimignano.

Hot tip: stay away from ZTL (Zona Traffico Limitato, or Limited Traffic Zone) areas. Highways are indicated by blue signboards, whereas toll roads are indicated by green signboards.

Bus from Florence to Tuscany

This is more my style of transportation because it's affordable and relieves my nervousness about swerving too much on the roadways. Several bus companies run in and around Tuscany from several hilltop towns and coastal districts (Siena, Grosseto, Cecina, Lucca, Pisa). The Florence bus station is located directly in front of the SMN train station. The bus schedules are available here.

Rail From Florence To Tuscany

The railway will restrict your travel options because many of the hilltop and seaside regions are inaccessible. But one of the most frequently traveled from Florence by train destinations in Siena.

You will travel a beautiful route to Siena, which is only 43 miles from Florence's center. Every hour, there are two trains available. Both trains stop at Empoli, where you can change to the other train that will take you to Siena. The train schedule is available here.

Organized Trips Between Tuscany And Florence

If you were curious about how I got from Florence to Tuscany, here was how.

Nothing calms my nerves like a well-planned tour with a knowledgeable guide leading the way, organizing my schedule, and handling all the details. I only needed to relax, take in the scenery, and enjoy the bus ride to take in the breathtaking Tuscan landscape!

Optimum Period To Visit Tuscany

Although Tuscany has pleasant weather all year long, mid-May to mid-July and the month of September is the finest times to visit. Tuscany's springtime boasts clear, sunny sky and temperatures that range from 64°F (18°C) to 82°F (28°C), making it the ideal season for sightseeing and taking advantage of the Tuscan sun. As it's also the busiest travel time of year, plan by making your hotel and airfare reservations to prevent price increases.

The fall months of October and November are ideal for travel to Tuscany because of the excellent weather. This is a fantastic time to visit Tuscany if the dates aren't important. Around this time, the area celebrates several holidays, including Easter and Harvest.

In Tuscany, the winter months of December through February are considered the low season. Tuscany offers many wonderful possibilities to ring in the holiday cheer and the new year, though, if the weather isn't an issue and you're in the holiday spirit and looking to celebrate Christmas. It is ideal for travelers who wish to avoid severe weather and cut their travel costs in half because there is little likelihood of snow.

Tuscan restaurants

Since the beginning of time, Tuscan chefs have been reaching new heights in the culinary world. Throughout Tuscany, several farm-to-table restaurants serve fusions of traditional cuisine with a dash of modernity. These restaurants serve the freshest and most authentic Italian cuisine. Here are our top selections for Tuscany's top eateries.

CONCLUSION

A distinctive fusion of art, culture, history, cuisine, wine, and scenic beauty can be found in Tuscany. There is something for everyone in Tuscany, from the picturesque towns and citics to the gently sloping countryside.

In this guide, we've outlined the top sights and activities in the area and given you expert advice on how to make the most of your visit.

Summary of the Best Attractions And Activities In Tuscany

Visit the best museums, galleries, and other cultural institutions in Tuscany, as well as take part in its festivals and events, to learn more about its history, art, and culture.

Enjoying Tuscany's beaches and coastline while hiking, motorcycling, or riding a horse through the region's natural parks and reserves.

seeing the best wineries, restaurants, and food markets in Tuscany, participating in cooking workshops, and tasting its finest wines.

selecting the ideal lodging in Tuscany, whether it be a chic bed & breakfast, a rustic farm, or a luxury hotel.

Final Tips and Suggestions For Visitors To Tuscany In 2023

To avoid crowds and excessive rates, try traveling in the shoulder seasons (April through May and September through October).

To tour Tuscany's countryside and smaller towns and villages, rent a car or employ a driver.

Before your journey, brush up on some fundamental Italian words to help you interact with people and fully experience the culture.

Because many of Tuscany's streets and towns are pedestrian-friendly, be prepared to walk and wear comfortable shoes.

Don't forget to try some of the area's delectable cuisine, which includes items like gelato, bistecca alla Fiorentina, and pasta with truffles.

In conclusion, tourists seeking to fully immerse themselves in Italy's rich culture and history can find a multitude of experiences in Tuscany.

You can maximize your travel opportunities and make lifelong memories in this breathtaking and distinctive region of the world by following our advice.